There's Still Time

There's Still Time

The Success of the Endangered Species Act

by Mark Galan with a foreword by Bruce Babbitt

NATIONAL GEOGRAPHIC SOCIETY

WASHINGTON, D.C.

With special thanks to Dave Etnier, University of Tennessee, and Bill Heinrich, The Peregrine Fund, and the caring people at the U.S. Fish and Wildlife Service: Ken Burton, Karen Day, Paul Hartfield, Gary Henry, Jan Knight, Tom Nesle, Bob Parenti, Molly Sperduto, and Gary Stolz.

Published by the
National Geographic Society
1145 17th Street N.W.
Washington, D.C. 20036

Reg Murphy
*President and
Chief Executive Officer*

Gilbert M. Grosvenor
Chairman of the Board

Nina D. Hoffman
Senior Vice President

William R. Gray
*Vice President,
Director of the Book Division*

Staff for this Book

Barbara Lalicki
*Director of Children's Publishing,
Editor*

Mark Galan
Writer

David M. Seager
Art Director

Barbara Brownell
Senior Editor

Susan A Franques
Illustrations Editor

Meredith D. Wilcox
Illustrations Assistant

Elizabeth MacRae-Bobynskyj
Indexer

Vincent P. Ryan
Manufacturing Manager

Lewis R. Bassford
Production Manager

Dale-Marie Herring
Staff Assistant

Illustrations credits: Front cover, Art Wolfe; Back cover (upper left), Art Wolfe; Back (upper right), Lynn M. Stone/DRK Photo; Back (lower), Robert & Jean Pollock/Biological Photo Service; 1, Jim Borrowman; 2-3, B. & C. Alexander/Photo Researchers; 6-7, John Shaw; 9, National Association of Audubon Societies; 10-11, T. A. Wiewandt/DRK Photo; 11, Sarah Leen; 12-13, Michio Hoshino/Minden Pictures; 14-15, Joel Sartore; 15, Tom McHugh/Photo Researchers; 16-17 (both), Joel Sartore; 18, Joel Sartore; 18 (inset), C. K. Lorenz/Photo Researchers; 19, Lynn M. Stone/DRK Photo; 20, Marty Cordano/ DRK Photo; 20-21, Art Wolfe; 22-23 (both), Galen Rowell; 24, William H. Mullins/Photo Researchers; 24-25, David Jensen; 25, Marianne Austin-McDermon; 26, Joel Sartore; 26 (inset), Richard T. Bryant; 27, Robert & Jean Pollock/Biological Photo Service; 28-29, Lon E. Lauber; 30, Jim Brandenburg/Minden Pictures; 30-31, Art Wolfe; 32, 32-33, C.C. Lockwood/DRK Photo; 33, Les Saucier, Photo/Nats; 34-35, Joel Sartore; 35, Alan D. Carey/Photo Researchers; 36-37, Kevin McDonnell/Mo Yung Productions; 37, Mildred Scholnick/Marine Mammal Images

Library of Congress CIP Data
Galan, Mark A.
    There's still time : the success of the endangered species act / foreword by Bruce Babbit ; written by Mark Galan.
       p.   cm.
    Includes index.
    ISBN 0-7922-4140-1
    1. Endangered species—United Sates.
I. National Geographic
Society (U.S.) II. Title.
QH76.G33 1997
333.95'22'0973—dc21   97-11564
                                                    CIP
                                                    AC

The Society is supported through membership dues and income from the sale of its educational products. Call 1-800-NGS-LINE for more information. Visit our website at www.nationalgeographic.com.

Distributed by Publishers Group West
For information call 1-800-788-3123

Printed in the United States of America
on recycled paper

ENDANGERED
MEANS THERE'S
Still Time.

Motto of the Fish and Wildlife Service

FOREWORD

BY BRUCE BABBITT

When youngsters at a Los Angeles "Eco-Expo" were asked to answer the basic question: "Why save endangered species?" Gabriel replied, "Because God gave us the animals." Travis and Gina wrote, "Because we love them." Another child answered, "Because they are a part of our life. If we didn't have them, it would not be a complete world."

Now, in my lifetime I have heard many, many political, agricultural, scientific, medical, and ecological reasons for saving endangered species. I have in fact hired biologists and ecologists for just that purpose. All their reasons have to do with providing humans with potential cures for disease, or yielding humans new strains of drought-resistant crops, or offering humans a biological remedy for oil spills. They give thousands

of reasons why species are useful to humans.

None of these reasons move me like the children's. For these children are putting in plain words a complex notion that has been lost or forgotten by many. The children's answers express the moral and spiritual belief that there may be a higher purpose inherent in creation, demanding our respect and our stewardship, quite apart from whether a particular species is or ever will be of material use to people.

Their answers remind us of important values.

I affirm that these values remain at the heart of the Endangered Species Act, that they make themselves manifest through the green eyes of the gray wolf, the call of the whooping crane, the splash of a trout, and the voices of America's children.

Why should we save endangered species? Let us answer this question with one voice, the voice of the child who replied: "Because we can."

INTRODUCTION

Although the United States Congress passed a number of laws early in the 20th century to help protect certain animals from overhunting, by the 1960s it was clear that much of America's wildlife was in big trouble. Rapid development and rampant pollution had taken their toll on many species. Decades of unrestricted hunting had caught up with others.

In 1966 a law called the Endangered Species Preservation Act created the country's first endangered species list, naming 109 animals that were on the verge of extinction.

Seven years later Congress passed the Endangered Species Act, which was a great improvement over the 1966 law. It didn't just identify species that were in danger—it enabled the government to take direct action to protect them. In addition to making it illegal to kill any plant or creature on the list, the government could also take preventative measures. For example, it could block construction on land that is home to an endangered species. Furthermore, for the first time plants and invertebrates were allowed on the list. This recognizes that it is important to preserve the wide diversity of life in the world—not just famous American species like the bald eagle.

The list also keeps track of endangered foreign species, such as the chimpanzee and the white rhinoceros. As a result of 1973's Convention on International Trade in Endangered Species of Wild Flora and Fauna (CITES), it is illegal to trade in endangered species worldwide. CITES helped slow down the poaching of endangered elephants, for example, when it banned the importation of ivory tusks in 1990.

It is the responsibility of the United States Fish and Wildlife Service to administer the Act and maintain the endangered species list.

The plants and animals on the endangered species list are classified in one of two ways: endangered, which means the species is in immediate peril of becoming extinct; and threatened, which means that the species is declining and may eventually face extinction unless something is done to help it.

If a threatened species continues to disappear its status can be changed to endangered. If an endangered species improves it can be "downlisted" to threatened. After downlisting, if a species continues to thrive it can be taken off the list completely, which has happened to such animals as the brown pelican and California gray whale. Any modifications to the list—additions, removals, or changes in status—require an act of Congress.

PASSENGER PIGEON

When America was young, it was home to as many as five billion passenger pigeons. Flocks were so huge that they blocked out the sun as they flew overhead. This abundance was a blessing for the people who settled the Great Plains. The pigeons seemed to provide a never-ending food supply. But the supply wasn't infinite. Over time, uncontrolled hunting took its toll.

As their numbers dwindled, the remaining population of pigeons became too small to support itself. There weren't enough pigeons left to breed successfully. By 1910 there was only one passenger pigeon left.

Nicknamed "Martha" by her caretakers at the Cincinnati Zoo, she died in 1914, proving that even a species that numbers in billions can be driven to extinction by our thoughtlessness.

BUFFALO

While passenger pigeons soared through the skies, over 60 million buffalo thundered across the Great Plains. There were enough buffalo to outweigh every person now alive in the United States and Canada. For hundreds of years Plains Indians had lived in harmony with these creatures, finding them a source of food, clothing, and spiritual comfort. But the building of the transcontinental railroad and the movement of settlers West spelled disaster for the buffalo. Hunted mercilessly, there were fewer than 300 left by 1900.

Fortunately buffalo did not die out like the passenger pigeon. Using a breeding stock from New York's Bronx Zoo, conservationists were able to repopulate the species, biologically known as American bison, and protect it from hunters. Nearly a century later the shaggy beasts number in the tens of thousands, and will probably never face extinction again.

BALD EAGLE

In 1782, Benjamin Franklin wanted the turkey, but America chose the bald eagle as its national bird. People liked its fierce, independent look. Back then there were as many as 75,000 eagles in what would become the continental U.S. But as the country was settled, much of the eagle's forest and wetland habitats were destroyed by development. The birds were hunted by ranchers as pests, and they suffered from lead poisoning when they fed on dead animals that had been killed with lead shot.

The most devastating blow to the eagle came after World War II, when farmers began using a pesticide called DDT on their crops. The DDT would wash into nearby lakes and streams where it was absorbed by plants and small animals, which were then eaten by fish. When eagles fed on the fish, the DDT would accumulate in their bodies and cause them to lay eggs that were too thin to protect the chicks inside. By the early 1960s, there were fewer than 450 nesting pairs of eagles in the lower 48 states. When the Endangered Species Act was passed in 1973, the bald eagle—along with 108 other species—was on the list.

But even before the Endangered Species Act, the government had taken action to protect its national symbol. In 1940 Congress made it illegal to kill bald eagles without a permit. And in 1972 the use of DDT was banned. Since then the eagle has staged a remarkable comeback, rebounding to over 5,000 nesting pairs in the continental U.S. (There are roughly 40,000 eagles in Alaska.) So promising is the eagle's recovery that in 1995 the U.S. Fish and Wildlife Service changed the status of the bald eagle from endangered to threatened.

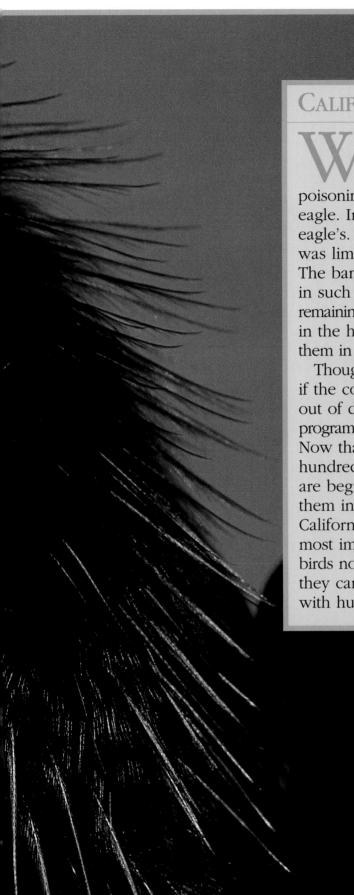

CALIFORNIA CONDOR

With a wingspan of nearly ten feet, the California condor is North America's largest flying bird. But its size was no protection against DDT, lead poisoning, and other factors that were killing the bald eagle. In fact this bird's plight was far worse than the eagle's. There were many fewer condors, and their range was limited to just a small portion of southern California. The ban on DDT helped, but by 1986, the condor was in such bad shape that all remaining birds were captured in the hopes of breeding them in captivity.

Though it's too soon to tell if the condor will ever be out of danger, the breeding program seems to be working. Now that there are about a hundred condors, biologists are beginning to release them into the wild in California and Arizona. The most important test these birds now face is whether they can share their habitat with humans.

RED WOLF

The red wolf was another one of the original 109 endangered species. Hunted relentlessly and squeezed by a shrinking habitat, these wolves numbered just 14 by the 1970s. The key to saving this species, as with the California condor, was captive breeding. Protected from harm in zoos, wolves have increased in number to about 350—enough to try releasing them into the wild.

There are now two experimental populations of wolves living in North Carolina and Tennessee, in Alligator River National Wildlife Refuge and Great Smoky Mountains National Park. Wildlife biologists are carefully monitoring the wolves' progress in both locations.

BROWN PELICAN

The brown pelican is one of the great success stories of the Endangered Species Act. This ungainly bird has few predators in the wild, but it was almost made extinct by people—those who hunted it for feathers, killed it as a nuisance, and stole its eggs. And since the pelican feeds almost exclusively on fish, it was ravaged by DDT.

In 1903, President Theodore Roosevelt created the Pelican Island National Wildlife Refuge in Florida—America's first wildlife refuge. This reduced the threat from hunters, until a law passed in 1918 banned pelican hunting everywhere. The pelican was also one of the first birds to rebound after the 1972 ban on DDT. In fact, the Atlantic coast population has done so well that in 1985 the Fish and Wildlife Service removed this group from the endangered species list. The pelican populations on the Gulf and Pacific coasts, while improving, remain on the list.

WHOOPING CRANE

The whooping crane is the tallest bird in North America, with an average height of $4\frac{1}{2}$ feet. Centuries ago whooping cranes ranged over most of the continent, from the Arctic to Mexico and from Utah to the Atlantic coast. Since then, their wilderness habitats have steadily shrunk. There were less than 20 birds left not long ago.

Captive breeding has helped the crane population rise to over 300 birds, most living in a single flock that migrates between Canada and Texas. A recently established second flock, ranging between Idaho and New Mexico, is struggling to survive. Biologists have turned to unusual strategies to restock these two populations. For instance, they give the eggs of captive whoopers to flocks of sandhill cranes to hatch and raise as "foster parents." When the chicks grow up, they seek out their own kind to breed.

ALLIGATOR

Scientists often refer to the alligator as a "living fossil," because it has survived virtually unchanged for the past 200 million years. But despite its long history on earth, the American alligator nearly disappeared because of overhunting. Once the Endangered Species Act prohibited killing them, the remaining alligators bred so quickly that the Fish and Wildlife Service declared them recovered in 1987.

It is still illegal to kill alligators, however, because they closely resemble the American crocodile—an endangered species. Because of this law, nobody can kill a crocodile and claim to have mistaken it for an alligator.

FALCON

One of the world's fastest birds, the Peregrine falcon can reach speeds of 200 miles per hour while diving for prey. These birds once lived throughout most of the country, but DDT eliminated peregrines from the eastern United States and reduced the western population to only 19 known pairs.

Through captive breeding and release programs, the Fish and Wildlife Service and private organizations such as The Peregrine Fund have brought the falcon back to the East and restored its numbers in the West. The birds have also helped their own cause by adapting to life in big cities, nesting atop skyscrapers and tall bridges.

MacFarlane's Four-o-Clock

In 1936 Ed MacFarlane, a boatman on the Snake River, pointed out a lavender flower to two of his passengers, both botanists. When they identified the plant as a new species, the botanists named it MacFarlane's four-o-clock in honor of their guide.

By 1947, MacFarlane's four-o-clock was believed to be extinct. Nobody could find even a single flower. Then it was rediscovered in the late '70s. Soon afterward, it was placed on the endangered species list. One of the first things biologists do when a species is listed as endangered is to look for it. When the species is found, its site can be protected from harm.

This is what saved MacFarlane's four-o-clock. Searchers found a number of previously unknown plant populations that were in danger of being trampled by grazing cattle. The flowers that exist on public property are now protected, and landowners are cooperating with the government to look after those that exist on private property.

LOCH LOMOND COYOTE THISTLE

The Loch Lomond coyote thistle, a plant related to parsley, lives within a single wetland area in northern California. In 1985 the owner of the land illegally dredged the area, which put the thistle in immediate danger of extinction. The Fish and Wildlife Service responded by giving it emergency protection as an endangered species—the Endangered Species Act allows officials to do this if a species is suddenly imperiled. This prevented the landowner from making any further alterations to the wetland area.

To protect the plant permanently, the California Department of Fish and Game purchased the land on which the thistle lives. In addition, biologists are currently trying to secure the land adjacent to the plant's habitat.

SNAIL DARTER

When the snail darter was discovered in a Tennessee river tributary in 1973, nobody thought the three-inch-long  fish would create such a controversy. But when the government wanted to build a dam across the Tennessee River, environmentalists sued because the dam would destroy the only stream in which the snail darter was known to exist. The case went all the way to the Supreme Court, which ruled in favor of saving the fish. Then Congress circumvented the ruling by passing a law that allowed the dam's construction.

Anticipating the destruction of the snail darter's habitat, biologists transplanted as many of the fish as they could to nearby streams. And they eventually found additional populations elsewhere in Tennessee, as well as in Georgia and Alabama. By 1984, the fish were doing well enough to be downlisted from endangered to threatened.

GREENBACK CUTTHROAT TROUT

Transplanting has also helped the greenback cutthroat trout, which lives in the rivers of central Colorado. Though the greenback faced threats from a shrinking habitat and increasing pollution, the major problem was competition from non-native fish like the brook trout and rainbow trout. Because brook trout reproduce faster and were eating most of the available food, the greenbacks found themselves crowded out of their own home. Interbreeding with rainbow trout has also been a problem.

After many foreign trout were removed and some of the greenbacks were taken to new streams, the greenback population eventually stabilized. They were downlisted from endangered to threatened in 1978, and if current populations remain stable, biologists hope to remove them from the list completely by the year 2000.

ALEUTIAN CANADA GOOSE

Competition from an introduced species nearly wiped out the Aleutian Canada goose, which lives on the westernmost portion of Alaska's Aleutian Island chain. The geese used to roam the entire chain but were killed on most islands by Arctic foxes, which were brought to the Aleutians by traders in the 1830s. By the mid-1970s there were only about 800 geese left. Efforts to remove as many foxes as possible, as well as captive breeding and reintroduction programs for the geese, have boosted the population to over 2,000.

The Aleutian goose was fortunate. It was threatened by a single predator, which could be removed from the habitat with relative ease. But some ecosystems are under siege from many non-native species at once. Nowhere is this a bigger problem than in Hawaii. There native plants are choked by plants brought from the mainland. They are also trampled and eaten by wild goats and pigs, descended from animals brought to the islands by settlers hundreds of years ago. And when the native forests go, the animals that live in them also die. Most can't adapt to life without the ecosystem they depend on for survival.

GRAY WOLF

The gray wolf, which grows larger than the red wolf, was virtually hunted out of existence in the eastern United States in the 19th century. And by 1930 the wolves were just about gone from the western part of the country as well, the result of a government-sponsored program to rid farmers and ranchers of the animals. Those left—roughly 2,000 of them—live in remote areas of the upper Midwest and Northwest. Some 6-7,000 wolves also live in Alaska, where they are not listed as endangered or threatened.

The Endangered Species Act has helped protect the remaining wolves. In return, government and private organizations reimburse ranchers when their animals are killed by wolves—something that happens far less frequently than people think. And efforts have been underway to reintroduce wolves to areas that have not seen them for decades, including Yellowstone National Park.

LOUISIANA PEARLSHELL MUSSEL

Though the best-known endangered species are large birds and mammals like condors and wolves, most of the species on the list are small and relatively unknown. An example is the Louisiana pearlshell mussel, one of almost 300 freshwater mussel species native to North America. Many of these mussels are endangered or threatened—or already extinct—because the clear, fast-moving streams they need to live in are being destroyed by dams and pollution.

The Louisiana pearlshell is an exception to this trend because most of these mussels happen to live on public land. To help protect the pearlshell, the government has restricted logging near the streams where the mussel lives. Furthermore, surveys have uncovered an additional pearlshell population, which is now also protected. With its numbers stable, the pearlshell was downlisted from endangered to threatened in 1993.

SMALL WHORLED POGONIA

The small whorled pogonia, which lives mostly in Maine and New Hampshire, is in constant danger of losing its forest habitat to development. But like many flowers that are small, beautiful, and rare, the pogonia is also threatened by collectors, who dig the flowers up and take them to their homes and labs. Some species of cactus in the Southwest and carnivorous plants of the Southeast, such as the Venus flytrap, are on the verge of extinction exactly for this reason. Collectors pose a special threat to the small whorled pogonia, because botanists believe that pogonias usually do not survive

being taken from the wild.

Pogonias are hard to find because they tend to grow individually, rather than in large groups. Despite this difficulty, survey teams have located a number of pogonia populations throughout the East and Midwest. These finds, which are protected and closely monitored, prompted the Fish and Wildlife Service to reclassify the flower as threatened in 1994.

BLACK-FOOTED FERRET

Sometimes it turns out that species are interconnected in ways we never realized. A good example of this is the relationship between the prairie dog and the black-footed ferret. For most of the 20th century farmers and ranchers on the Great Plains systematically killed prairie dogs, because the burrows they dug were a hazard to farm animals. But as the prairie dog population fell so did the population of black-footed ferrets, which feed on them. By 1979 the ferret was feared extinct.

A ferret population was discovered in 1981, though it dwindled from disease to just 18 six years later. At that point biologists captured all of them for captive breeding

programs, and their numbers have slowly climbed ever since. Ferrets have been reintroduced to the wild in Wyoming, Montana, South Dakota, and Arizona, and so far appear to be adapting well to their new homes.

GRAY WHALE

Although gray whales disappeared from the North Atlantic Ocean about 200 years ago, the California gray whale has staged a remarkable comeback. In the 1970s there were only about 12,500 of the massive creatures. But when the whale was declared recovered and taken off the endangered species list in 1994, there were almost twice as many, a number roughly equal to how many there were before the whaling industry began killing them off in the 19th century.

In addition to receiving protection through the Endangered Species Act, marine species like whales are also protected by other laws, such as the Marine Mammal Protection Act— and the Federal government will often try to reach agreements with other countries to stop or curb the taking of endangered species that live in international waters.

The Endangered Species Act has helped save plants and animals. But for each one that has recovered there are many others that teeter on the edge of extinction. Scientists speculate that each day, at least one of the about 1.75 million known species on earth vanishes. Habitat destruction, competition from non-native species, disease, and excessive hunting have combined to put these species in peril.

The most important steps we can take in preserving species diversity involve research and education. The more we know about any form of life, the better we can help it survive. Research can also help us identify new species—there may be as many as 30 million of them waiting to be discovered—before ecological pressures drive them into extinction.

The fate of the world's plants and animals rests on how well we can balance the needs of humans with the needs of wildlife. In this effort, the successes of the Endangered Species Act leave us grateful—and aware that there is much that still can be done.

INDEX